A Recovery Journal
For Exploring
Who I Am

A Recovery Journal
For Exploring
Who I Am

HAZELDEN®

Hazelden
Center City, Minnesota 55012-0176

ISBN: 0-89486-935-3

About the workbook:

For those recovering from an addiction, keeping a journal can be an emotional outlet and an avenue for personal growth, as well as a trip into uncharted territory—sometimes intimidating, frequently uncomfortable, yet always rewarding.

A Recovery Journal for Exploring Who I Am explains the concept behind journaling, describes how to set up and use a journal, and provides guidelines for making a journal a valuable element in the recovery process. Simply yet knowledgeably written, this workbook encourages the reader to discard old, nonproductive attitudes about what a writer is and what "good" writing involves. More important, *A Recovery Journal* helps to make that first step—putting pen to paper—easier for everyone who reads it.

Introduction

Congratulations. You've picked up this workbook because you've made some courageous changes in your life. You've chosen recovery over addiction. That decision is one of life's turning points.

This workbook was designed for people recovering from addiction, whether as inpatients or outpatients, but it's not a book about recovery. It's a workbook about writing. It offers recovering people instruction on how to use writing as a method of self-reflection. We may dismiss journal writing as an option because we're afraid that our writing won't be "good." But we'll discover in this workbook that each of us has the ability to write about our own lives.

Most of the exercises and writing ideas you'll find here can be done right in the workbook. For some, you may need more paper. Let's hope this workbook will inspire you to find a big fat empty notebook to use as a journal—that's how much you'll enjoy writing!

The workbook is divided into several sections. The first section explains how journal writing and recovery can work together. The second section helps dispel some myths about writing by showing how much writing ordinary people do all of the time. We enter the world of observation in the third section, where the exercises are designed to increase our awareness of how we interact with our physical surroundings. From there, we move to more internal concerns and discover how writing can help us work through stress and anxiety. In the fifth section, we'll discover something called "writer's memory" and learn how to use memory as a resource for writing. The workbook concludes with a glimpse toward tomorrow and leaves us learning how to create a vision for our future.

Before you begin, it's important to remember to use this workbook as just one of the many resources available to you as a recovering person. No one source provides all of the answers. This workbook can't replace friends, counselors, or Twelve Step groups. What it can do is introduce you to journal writing as one part of your recovery program. An important part. You'll be writing your story.

Good luck!

CHAPTER ONE

The Journey of Writing

Uncharted territory.

That's what we're entering right now. Recovering from any type of addiction is a new experience. We're making changes in our daily behavior. Our routines and habits are open to scrutiny. New thoughts and emotions erupt. We're beginning to face the unexplored emotional territory within ourselves. We want to free ourselves from addiction.

For many of us, living a life of sobriety or abstinence will be an unfamiliar, and sometimes frightening, experience. We find ourselves in a treatment program because addiction has taken over our life. What does it mean to live without alcohol, drugs, food, or sex as the driving force in life? These were the things that gave our lives meaning and purpose. Sober or abstinent, we will find ourselves without the structure that addiction provided. We will be faced with realities of life that we've pushed away: strong emotions, money we need to earn to live, friendships we've let deteriorate, bills left unpaid, memories.

Uncharted territory.

Who wouldn't find themselves feeling alone and afraid on such a journey? Of course, as the Twelve Step program tells us, we're really not as alone as we may sometimes feel. There are support communities all around us—from people who may be with us in treatment centers, to our local Twelve Step group, to people recovering in the thousands of support groups across the country. Most important, our Higher Power is with each of us all the time. It is there where we find courage, strength, and comfort.

Still, we may feel alone. People surround us—and we're discovering that the presence of our Higher Power is a constant source of strength—but in order to communicate with other people and to feel the support and energy of our Higher Power, we must be able to make connections, to bridge that gap between ourselves and others. To communicate with our Higher Power, we need to reach into ourselves. We need to tap into the peace and self-knowledge that our Higher Power can lead us to. This is an inward journey.

In fact, even communicating with other people requires an inward journey, a certain amount of self-reflection. The best communication requires honesty and a continuing search for self-awareness. This isn't a one-day endeavor. It's a process. We need to develop a new relationship with ourselves at the same time that we develop relationships with others. This requires an inward journey. This requires self-awareness.

Uncharted territory.

So how do we explore this territory? Journaling.

The very word may send us running. Journaling! That means writing. Most people, from professors to schoolchildren, have a certain amount of fear about writing. There's the risk of self-exposure. (What if someone reads it and sees that I'm an awful writer? Even worse, what if someone finds out all my secrets, discovers who I really am?) This is the greatest secret of all: We've been hiding for a long time, hiding from ourselves and from other people.

What if we *do* discover ourselves? Actually, that's the whole point. We *do* want to uncover our secrets, the unknown within ourselves. So before panic overtakes us, let's take a step back, forget the word *writing*, and look at what we're really concerned about: exploring uncharted territory and making discoveries. A journal is simply a tool for doing this.

Think about the phrase "exploring uncharted territory." It sounds like the "Star Trek" theme—going where no man or woman has gone before! That's exactly what we're doing when we begin discovering ourselves. We're each unique. But while the territory differs, we're not alone as explorers. All around us, many people are embarking on similar journeys into themselves. Also, people have been exploring different types of uncharted territories, and writing about their explorations, for centuries.

The original explorers were ship captains, pioneers, and sailors. There was a time when the earth's landscape was unexplored. The individual oceans and continents had yet to be named, to be mapped out and understood. The sailors and pioneers who explored the earth kept journals of their travels. How else could they record and remember the details of the landscape? Not only did they want to chart, or write about, new territory, but they also needed to be able to find their way back home. Look at the words *journal* and *journey*. They share the same root and a common origin—a journal is simply a written account of a journey. Travelers have been keeping journals for centuries.

This is what we will be doing. We too are travelers. The difference is that the journey we're embarking on is an interior one. But that doesn't mean we don't need maps and records! As people accustomed to the familiar landscape of addiction, we find the landscape of our interior lives is not only foreign, but perhaps frightening. We need records, notes, and information to find our way home, just like the first explorers did. We need to map out and understand the way our interior world works so that we don't get lost. Home, to us, is where we're headed.

A life governed by addiction is being lost. We're embarking on a homeward course.

This workbook will become an account of our individual journeys; it is a place to learn how to record and map our journey of recovery. There's no specific destination. We won't wake up one day and say, "I'm there." This journey doesn't end, because we're each constantly discovering and rediscovering ourselves as we change and grow. However, the more accustomed we become to traveling, the less frightening and more exciting the journey becomes.

Let's look at the beginning of one person's journey.

> I want to write this now while I'm feeling and thinking and knowing so I can read this days and months—even years—from now and remember (at least some, anyway) of the feeling of this time.
>
> I feel "baseless." Everything is in a state of transition. Yesterday I felt utterly lost and alone, like it was just me in tis foreign, cold hospital with no one who know or wondered about how or what I was feeling. It's like I go around all day long, fitting my body into the scheduled activities but my mind and my heart, my *spirit* simply isn't there.

This is the first entry in the journal of someone in treatment for an eating disorder. Let's get picky about words. There are a couple of mistakes in grammar. The writer left out the *h* in *this*. Someone well trained in English would probably tell us that the punctuation isn't right, either. This is *not* perfect writing.

And that doesn't matter. What does matter is that this person is describing feelings and does it very well. Don't we all know that feeling, that our body is sitting in a room, but some essential part of us—mind or spirit—just isn't there? The writer of this piece is lonely, empty, and scared. This may not be a particularly "happy" beginning to her journey of recovery, but that's okay. It's an accurate account of exactly where she really is.

Where are you, what are you feeling, right now? Take a few minutes to find out. After you read this, close your eyes and focus on your chest, stomach, head. Do you feel tight? Is it hard to relax? Fear, anger, joy, hope— what can you pinpoint inside yourself? If you can't capture an emotion or think of the right word, don't worry. Just think of some words that describe how you feel. After you spend some time feeling what's inside of your body, write down what you've discovered.

_____

_____

_____

_____

_____

_____

_____

_____

Now read what you've written, without judgment. It doesn't matter if the grammar isn't right or some words are misspelled. Punctuation isn't important, either. The important thing is learning to identify and record information about ourselves and the world around us.

In this workbook, writing is simply a tool for self-discovery. It's how we identify where we are in our personal journey of recovery. Writing will become a way of charting new territory within ourselves. All sorts of other people can help guide us through this journey: doctors, counselors, other recovering people, perhaps family and friends. These people provide essential support and guidance. But it is up to each of us, individually, to keep track of where we've been, where we are now, and where we're going.

Writing is a great way to record what is happening in our lives. Writing can also be used as a tool to lead us in directions that we want to go. Sounds great, you may be saying, but I'M NOT A WRITER! Oh yeah? Read on.

WRITING IDEAS

1. Remember the sample journal entry presented earlier in this chapter? You can do the same thing. If you're in treatment now, or have been in the past, return to memories of the first day. Who checked you in and showed you to your room? Is it autumn—crisping brown leaves piling outside of the bedroom window? What sorts of smells are in the air? What are you wearing? Maybe you're feeling optimistic and excited, perhaps a little tired and scared. Write down each memory. Don't worry about putting words in

exactly the right place. This is simply information that you can refer back to—two days or ten years from now—in order to see exactly where you started.

_____

_____

_____

_____

_____

_____

_____

_____

2. If you haven't been in a treatment program, try to return to memories of your first day of sobriety or abstinence. Were you tense, anxious? Perhaps you felt relief or even joy. Recall the weather, people, and activities. Try to re-create, in writing, the entire scene and feeling of that day.

_____

_____

_____

_____

_____

_____

_____

_____

3. Make a record of one day's activities. Don't worry about creating perfect sentences; just carry a notebook around and jot down what happens.

Record the events of each hour. Keep track of the conversations you have. Describe how your friend looked while you watched TV together. Pinpoint a word or two that captures your predominant attitude or emotion. Maybe you're nervous at 10:00 A.M., angry by noon, and then relaxed and calm around 3:00 P.M.

Keep the entries brief. This is an exercise in the *habit* of awareness. You're beginning to develop the habit of noticing your surroundings and how you react to them.

4. Why did you pick up this workbook on journaling? Perhaps a particular need was tugging at the edges of your mind. Maybe you've always wanted to be a writer or you wanted to find a structured approach to self-reflection.

Think about the point you're at in recovery. What issues are most pressing? Describe any new feelings or ideas that have begun to circulate. There may be new goals in your life. Summarize where you are in your journey of recovery.

_____

_____

_____

_____

_____

_____

_____

_____

_____

_____

_____

_____

CHAPTER TWO

Finding the Writer Within

Remember those original explorers we were talking about—sailors and pioneers recording voyages across new territory? People are still exploring new territories today: Astronauts keep journals and records; researchers exploring the bottom of the ocean floor take elaborate notes.

If we were to ask them, sailors, pioneers, and astronauts probably wouldn't define themselves as writers. We generally define ourselves in terms of our relationships to other people (husband, sister, friend) or how we earn our living (lawyer, cab driver, teacher). Almost every occupation requires some type of writing. A teacher makes a lesson plan; a waitress scribbles an order. They probably wouldn't include writing as part of their identities or as one of their job responsibilities. But they each write. Writing marks their progress and allows them to chart out their next tasks.

Stop reading for a minute and look directly to your left, over your shoulder. In one sentence, write down what you see.

_____
_____
_____

_____

_____

_____

_____

_____

Now take a good long look at your fingernails. Are they long, maybe painted pale pink? Or are the nails short stubs, sprouting hard white hangnails or revealing nervous bite marks? Touch them. Are your nails smooth or bumpy or dry? Write about your fingernails.

_____

_____

_____

_____

_____

You've just made two important types of observations. First, you noticed the environment—your physical surroundings. This wasn't an elaborate observation, just one quick sentence. Still, if you hadn't been planning to write about what was over your left shoulder, would you have noticed it at all? Would you have looked?

The second observation is about yourself. You took a look at one part of your body. How often during the day do you normally stop to scrutinize your fingernails? When we plan to record what we see, we generally start looking longer and harder at ourselves and at the world around us.

Have you ever heard the phrase "Take note of this" as someone points out broken glass on the road or directs your attention to an important memo at work? Think about that phrase, "Take note." We notice things, we make notations—we write about what we see. What we're trying to see now is our journey of recovery. We're observing and taking notes. Writing.

That's what you just did. *You can write.*

There's that awful word again—*write*. How many of us would boldly proclaim to the world, "I write!" Unfortunately, we attach a lot of unnecessary significance to the word *write*. Try for a minute to forget everything you've learned about writing. Erase those red pen marks that appeared on your grade school essays. Block out images of Ernest Hemingway or Shakespeare. Writing is just another activity that makes up the *ordinary* business of life. Think about driving. Most of us drive cars, trucks, or motorcycles. Driving is just something that we do to get us from one place to another. It's a skill we learn and improve with practice. We wouldn't cringe from saying "I can drive" or suddenly feel shy about calling ourselves drivers.

Writing is a lot like driving. There's nothing magical or mystical about it. It's a skill that we learn. Our driving improves with practice and time—so will our writing. What we need to do is shake off the images that circulate around the word *writing*. Those mistaken images tell us that only famous authors are writers and that harsh critics will swoop down and highlight mistakes with angry red ink.

What have you written in the past week? Perhaps you've sketched out a treatment plan, written a letter to a friend, or made some notes to yourself at work. You've done a couple of exercises in this workbook. *You can write. You're doing it now.* It's surprising how much writing we each do. In fact, we write so often that we don't even stop to think about it. We just make out the grocery list or scribble a message on a telephone pad. Go over the past week in your mind. What have you written? Count everything—telephone messages, thank-you cards, lists.

_____

_____

_____

_____

_____

We're all writers.

But what about those images we were discussing: red ink screaming at our mistakes, memories of junior high school English classes, and the picture of Shakespeare that shows who the *real* writer is? Let's tackle that red ink first. Look around you. Do you see anybody racing toward this workbook with a red pen? Is there a friend crouching around some corner waiting to rip apart your words? Of course not. That critic we're afraid of is ourselves! There's a slogan common among people who make their living as writers: Writers are their own worst critics.

Have you heard that phrase before? Maybe people have said something similar about you. As people with an addiction, we have a tendency to beat ourselves up. We may be quick to criticize ourselves each time we see our behavior as less than perfect. Sometimes we describe ourselves in terms of faults and shortcomings. We're our own worst critics.

So we need to be extra careful about judging our writing. It's common for people to dislike their own writing. We're taught to look for mistakes in school. Our papers are marked with what we've done wrong, instead of what we've done well. As a result, most people look at their writing and see only mistakes. In addition to sharing this learned attitude toward writing, as recovering people we may be unusually critical about *everything* we do!

That's why there's one rule for using this workbook: We will never judge our writing. Instead of looking for mistakes and focusing on what we don't like, we're just going to practice. The only audience we're writing for is *ourselves*. While we're in recovery, writing is a tool for self-discovery. That's it.

Think about tools: hammers, wrenches, screwdrivers. We might struggle to twist a big screw with a small screwdriver. When we realize we've made a mistake by selecting the wrong tool, we don't drop the tool in horror and shame. Instead, we simply acknowledge that the task requires a different screwdriver. We generally wouldn't reprimand ourselves for being bad or sloppy because we picked up the wrong tool. We just find the right one. The goal is to get that screw tightly secured.

Our goal with writing is to find the words that mark our progress of recovery. The more we practice writing, the more comfortable with this tool we'll become. It's amazing what can happen when we stop agonizing that we're not Shakespeare and throw away all of those red pens our minds still hold. Taking away all the pressure for perfection gives our minds the freedom they need to create.

Self-criticism blocks the truly great writing we can each do. Fear of *what* we may write can also block us. Again, people in recovery share fears and anxieties about writing that are common to most people. However, we may have a more complex kind of fear about writing. First, there's the fear that how we write isn't very good. Second, we may be anxious about the content of our writing. This anxiety can stem from the shame and guilt we may feel about addiction. Third, we're afraid that what we're writing about—recovery, addiction, our inner life—is something to be ashamed of.

We have not led "perfect" lives. There are events and emotions that are difficult to recall, let alone record. It's difficult to delve into ourselves. However, facing our fears is the best way to overcome them. No matter what our pasts have been, we have no need to stick with the shame. Perhaps the example of one man who dared to face the pain of his past can help us as we consider the prospect of facing the pain of our own.

One of the original journalers discussed in the beginning of this section was John Newton, the captain of a slave ship. For years, he transported people from Africa to be sold as slaves in America. One day he experienced a transformation. Perhaps he met the eye of a man in shackles or looked a woman captive full in the face. Something changed. He suddenly saw his occupation as a crime against humanity. Capturing people? Selling human beings? He turned his ship around and brought his cargo of people home.

Sailing back to Africa, Newton found himself faced with the task of charting this new course. It was a course directed by his heart. In his journal, he wrote about his pain. Unbearable anguish poured into his words. Ultimately, he wrote a poem about changing his course. He wrote about the great change within himself—a change that "saved a wretch like me." In his personal journal, that ordinary man wrote a poem that became one of our country's most cherished hymns—"Amazing Grace."

What was Newton thinking when he wrote those words? He wasn't thinking about fame. He probably wasn't comparing himself to the famous writers of his time. He certainly wasn't chewing his pen, muttering, "*Wretch!* What a bad word. I don't even know how to spell it, so I won't use it." If he had been doing those things (the kind of self-criticism we're accustomed to), the song "Amazing Grace" might never have been written.

What was Newton thinking about? He was reflecting on his personal journey. Words were tools to express the torment he felt. He didn't write *despite* his pain, he bravely wrote directly *from* that pain. He had the strength to face what he was feeling and to put those feelings on paper. The words of "Amazing Grace" are a map of what was happening within his heart.

We share this captain's courage. It is possible to honestly explore and write about our own lives. The most astonishing territory lies within ourselves. Unimaginable riches wait within each of us to be explored. We don't need to feel ashamed about the content of our writing any more than we should feel ashamed about the content of our hearts. Self-reflection produces rich writing. Examine yourself honestly, kindly, and compassionately.

WRITING IDEAS

1. Examine yourself for virtues and successes. What accomplishments are you proud of? Try to think in terms of everyday life. Maybe you're proud of newly discovered assertiveness. Perhaps the neat front lawn and always-clean living room reflect your personal discipline. Look for the small, everyday good things that you do. Too often, we overlook these and focus on what we could be doing better. What are you doing well right now?

_____

_____

_____

_____

2.   Here's a short exercise that will help you see the changes you've made in your thinking. Start with the phrase "I used to believe . . . but now I believe . . ." and fill in the blanks. For example, you might write, "I used to believe that I was lazy. Now I believe I am disciplined and responsible."

Spend some time describing, in detail, your old belief. Write about when the belief changed and why. Is the new belief an improvement?

_____

_____

_____

_____

_____

_____

_____

You can do this exercise over and over with different topics. Have your beliefs about politics, money, relationships, or education changed? What about beliefs about yourself?

_____

_____

_____

_____

_____

_____

_____

_____

CHAPTER THREE

Observation: Watch the World Unfold

No matter how many encouraging words about honesty and self-reflection we hear, looking inside of ourselves can be a daunting task. If we're not sure what's going on inside of ourselves, how can we write about it?

This is where we turn those ideas around. Here's the traditional belief: We understand ourselves first, and then we write out of this understanding. But we're going to allow writing to come first. Writing is a tool to help us increase self-knowledge. Right now, we're a little confused and wary. Beginning to let go of an addiction throws us off balance. We don't know *what* we think, *how* we feel. Who are we without an addiction?

Writing can direct us. Let's start. Take out a piece of blank paper. You can use the back of a worksheet or letter; just make sure one side is completely empty. Now write. That's the only instruction you have. When you've finished, come back to this workbook. Don't read the next paragraph until you've finished the exercise.

Pretty intimidating, isn't it? That was a broad assignment. Write *what*? It's amazing how one piece of paper can suddenly wipe our minds clean. We sit with a fresh, blank notebook and pick up a pen. Suddenly, we're blank too—no ideas, nothing. Sometimes this is called "writer's block." It's as if there's a brick wall somewhere inside of ourselves, cutting off all of the thoughts that normally crowd our brains.

However, the real problem isn't lack of something to say. The real cause of an inability to begin writing is that there's too much to say! Just now, when you stared at that piece of paper and slowly, carefully, began writing, the instructions probably didn't prove helpful. You were given only one word: *write*.

There are so many things to write about! There's the young manager in your office who chews purple bubble gum all day. Its sweet, sticky smell shoots through each room she enters. What about the pen you're using now?

It's a smooth, white cylinder with blue ink. Then there's this jumpy feeling in your stomach. Is it nerves, excitement, or withdrawal? That's something to write about. Don't forget the breakfast cereal you ate this morning. The soggy oat flakes turned the milk murky gray. The national deficit probably needs more stuff written about it. There are probably a few movie stars to fantasize about, too.

Get the picture? It's not that we have nothing to say, but that we have too much to say! Without any specific directions, the word *write* can mean "write anything and everything." As most of us know, when we're overwhelmed, we sometimes shut down and feel nothing. See nothing. Write nothing. We can't take on all of the problems in our lives in a single sitting. We certainly can't write about *everything* at once, either. It's time to narrow our focus.

So we're going to focus. We'll concentrate on observation. Observing is what we do when we begin to notice (remember "Take note of"?) the details of the world around us. Look around. What observations can you make about the room that you're in now? Spend a few minutes observing and recording those observations.

Did you take in the size of the room and the color of the carpet? Maybe it's a large room, designed for groups. There's a brown table with four swivel chairs and a TV. Did you write down things that you hadn't really "seen" before? Being asked to make observations tends to make us look harder. Perhaps you noticed that the keys on the old piano in the corner are cracking and yellow. That pattern on the carpet looked like big streaky zigzags at first, but it's really tiny little dots close together.

We live in a very visual world. Lots of our information and entertainment comes from television, movies, and magazines. Generally, we learn from looking—at chalkboards, instruction manuals for VCRs, pamphlets. You're looking at this workbook and using your eyes to learn about journaling right now.

But how does this book feel? Is it hard or soft? Does the cover have a slightly grainy feeling, or is it smooth, like a photograph? Hold it flat against your bare arm. Is this a different experience? Smell it. Is it that sort of woodsy, pulpy scent of new paper, or does the workbook smell stale? There's a little dust gathering along its edges. Drop the workbook to the floor. Maybe it makes a slapping sound, or a dull thud if it's falling on carpet. Take some time now and make observations about this workbook, using senses other than sight.

This was a very small assignment, just one little book. Nothing very aromatic or colorful, like a vase of freshly cut flowers. Nothing very big, but chances are that in the few short minutes you just spent sniffing and touching (and maybe tasting!) this workbook, you got a lot of new information. It's possible to "look" with our whole bodies, to see with more than our eyes.

Of course, just as we can't write about everything, we'll never be able to observe each little detail around us. But the more we practice, the more adept we'll become at taking in all kinds of information. The more aware we are and the more information we have, the better able we will be to understand and direct the course of our lives. When observing our own lives, we can taste, touch, smell, hear, see, think, and feel. We can use all of our senses to gather information in many different ways. Our bodies are standing in the middle of an explosion of experience!

Let's return to the observations you made about the room you're in. Did you use all of your senses in "looking" at the room? Does the room have a distinct smell? Perhaps a faint rose scent lingers from a can of air freshener. Voices drift in from people down the hall. The air feels dry, and stale dust tickles your throat. What additional details can you pick up when consciously using all of your senses? Every room has its own feeling or flavor.

Sink into the feeling of the room you're in. Even if there's nothing to taste, try to think in terms of flavor. Spend a few minutes describing the feeling or flavor of the room.

_____

_____

_____

_____

_____

Some of the observations you just made probably weren't too surprising. The furniture is familiar. You've already noticed the four large windows or the color of the walls. But thinking in terms of flavor may be a new experience. Normally, we don't use words describing taste or touch for what we see or hear. But it's possible to use words in unexpected ways. This can allow us to express more accurately what we're experiencing. Using everyday words in new ways can be particularly helpful when we're casting about for words that describe new feelings and experiences.

Sometimes the tiny details of each day seem like new experiences. We're simply not accustomed to seeking out subtleties. We're not used to smelling rooms or tasting workbooks. But what about tasting tea? How many different types of tea have you tasted? We tend to think about tea in terms of taste: sharp mint, soothing cinnamon, or cool lemon. But tea comes in different colors and textures, too. Can you recall what your favorite tea looks like? How would you describe its smell or the way tea leaves feel in your hand?

We don't stop to carefully scrutinize tea. We're not accustomed to savoring these small details of life. Big, bold events grab our attention— most of us have probably been mesmerized by a sinking red sun. But sunsets are predictable. That doesn't mean they're not gorgeous, simply that they happen every evening. We can't help noticing when half the sky changes color! Mint tea, on the other hand, is a subtle, small, sensory experience. While these subtle explosions of experience may take some work to really notice, they can be just as rewarding as the larger ones.

Sunsets and mint tea are examples of the large and small details of our environments that mesh together to give each day a unique feeling. There's a word we can use to help pinpoint the combined effect of all these big and small details. That word is *texture*. Let's look at what *The American Heritage*

Dictionary has to say about *texture*: "the appearance of a fabric resulting from the woven arrangement of its yarns or fibers; the composition or structure of a substance." Our lives have composition and structure. Days are composed of, or structured by, the things we do. Routines and activities structure our lives. We eat breakfast, go to work, attend a meeting in the evening. The details—cold sleeting rain, the smell of freshly peeled oranges, an eager hug from a friend—fill each activity to give our days a unique feeling. Everything meshes to weave the unique texture of each day.

Think about your morning routine. From the time you stumbled out of bed until you broke for lunch at noon, what were the activities and routines that structured your morning? Perhaps you took a shower, ate breakfast, read the paper, attended a Twelve Step meeting, or went to work. How about conversations with people? Remember what happened this morning and write it down.

_____

_____

_____

_____

_____

This is the structure of your morning. Now, try for the small details. If you ate breakfast, were the eggs runny or did the yolks stand firm when your fork cut into them? Remember the exact color of the morning sky. If you went to work, was the receptionist at your office cheerful and warm? Maybe the office was chaotic, and he barely had time for hello. Return to the feeling of the morning. Remember as many details as possible and write them all down.

_____

_____

_____

_____

_____

These details combine to make the structure of your day a textured experience. Maybe the perfect eggs, powder-blue sky, and cheerful receptionist combined to make the morning bright and upbeat. But if breakfast was bad, the air thick with fog, and the office gloomy, the morning may have seemed thick and gloomy, too. Now list some words that describe the texture of your morning.

_____

_____

_____

Was it hard to come up with the right words? There are all kinds of possibilities: *smooth, rough, fast, tense, soothing,* or *rocky.* Even though the number of words we could use is almost endless, it's still sometimes hard to find the "right" ones. Most of us have been trained to think there's a perfect writing style that our work should live up to.

Remember our discussion about writing earlier in this book? There's nothing magical about writing. And there isn't one perfect word! Words aren't good or bad. They're tools. Sometimes we find words that express what we feel and sometimes we don't. Mostly, we find words that are adequate, even if they don't exactly hit upon the meaning we want.

So there aren't "right" or "wrong" words. Of course, we know there are rules of grammar. But we're not concerned with those rules in this workbook. We're looking for words to locate our place in the journey of recovery. It's impossible for us to know right away what those words are, because each day of recovery is a new experience. We need to thrash around a little to figure out *how* we feel. It's good to experiment, to allow ourselves to try all kinds of words to find some that fit our new feelings.

Words are versatile tools. The same word or phrase can have different meanings. We've already talked about a new way of using the word *texture.* It refers to the feeling of material, as well as to the feeling of a particular time or place. Using the idea of texture in this way hinges on the word *feeling.* We feel material. We feel tension. We feel happy. We feel sand between our toes.

Think about what definitions in the dictionary look like. Three or four different meanings are given for nearly every word! In *The American Heritage Dictionary,* the word *form* has fourteen meanings as a noun and seven as a verb! That's twenty-one definitions for one very little, very ordinary word! What *form* means depends on how it's used in a sentence. There are many, many ways we can use the word *form.* So we don't need to get stuck searching for words that are perfect. Words are fluid. We're free to arrange them in entirely new ways as we search for the meaning that most accurately expresses what we want to say.

The search for words and the interior journey of recovery go hand in hand. Think about how hard it can be to find the words that best express what we feel. Generally, we first try familiar words. "I felt bored yesterday." No, that isn't exactly it. "I was tired yesterday." Not quite right, either. "Lonely?" That still isn't precise enough. Suddenly, you think of the word *vacant*. "I felt vacant yesterday." That's it! Of course, *vacant* isn't usually associated with people. Houses are vacant, empty, unoccupied. They're boarded up and abandoned.

Those images can also fit people! We feel empty, closed tight, with nothing to occupy our minds or hearts or time. But there's also longing and room to be filled—perhaps by contact with another person. Houses aren't meant to be vacant; they're built for people to live in. We're usually not comfortable when we feel vacant, either. Can you see how well those images work for both houses and people?

Trying different arrangements of words to describe complex feelings can help us pinpoint the exact nature of those feelings. Throw in words and see if they fit. Experiment. Expand the vocabulary that you have for feelings. Use words that apply to the condition of other things—the evening sky, an abandoned house, a blooming garden—to *your* condition or mood. Use words that describe the texture of bricks, velvet, or pudding to describe the texture of a day.

How does all this fit into our journeys of recovery? Why should we puzzle over a morning's texture and try to come up with descriptive words? Perhaps many of us have heard the phrase "the fabric of a life." That phrase refers to the quality and content of an individual life. The fabric of a life is its general tone, its feeling. A life can be woven together with chaos and crisis; a life can be colored by honesty and grace.

How could we describe the fabric of our lives so far? It may have been rocky. Addiction controlled the course of our days. Addiction numbed many of us to the details our senses provided. Instead of weaving a rich, varied life, addictive behavior dulls the edges of existence and limits experiences and routines to those that center around addiction.

But texture changes over time. Life has become richer and more complex. Our relationships with other people are growing stronger, and we feel emotions more directly. Free from addiction, we're rediscovering the pleasures of the physical world. We're also discovering who we are in that world. Addiction cut us off from all kinds of relationships. Now we're developing stronger relationships with other people, with ourselves, and with the physical world. And we're starting the process of finding the words we need to express all of the changes we're making!

WRITING IDEAS

1. Play with words! Here's a little writing trick related to our earlier discussion about the fluidity of words. Common words in uncommon combinations can create unexpectedly vivid meanings. For example: "Jeff stayed on the couch the whole afternoon, wrapped in gray silence." Gray silence? Since when is silence a color? But gray brings images to mind— maybe somberness or gloom. Using the word *gray* tells us that Jeff may be unhappy; perhaps he's warning people not to go near him. Here are some examples of ordinary words in unusual combinations: noisy color, creaking smile, musty gesture, darkening face, tangy words, bitter effort, waxy yawn, sleepy sunset.

   Now try to create your own combinations. See if these words can be used to describe your feelings.

   _____

   _____

   _____

   _____

2. Spend one day sniffing. Smell everything and write about it. Does each room in your house or treatment center have its own smell? What about the desk in the bedroom—the drawers? Smell your car, the air outside, carrots cooking. Experiment with things you don't normally smell, like freshly bathed skin, books, or kitchen cabinets.

   Over the next few days, focus on one of the other senses each day: taste, touch, sight, hearing. Use words normally associated with sight to help you describe things you hear or taste. Try words used for taste to describe how things feel when you touch them. Experiment with words while you explore your senses.

   _____

   _____

   _____

   _____

   _____

3.   Take time to really scrutinize your face. Normally, we peer into mirrors to apply makeup, shave, or check for food caught in our teeth. This time, don't check for flaws; just take note of what you see. Stand close to a mirror. Move your eyes slowly over your face. Is your face long, square, or round? Perhaps the skin is dry and your jaw line juts out clearly.

Describe what you see without using words that judge or evaluate attractiveness. Stare at the pupils of your eyes. Check for flecks of color; note the contour of the iris. Nose, mouth, cheekbones, forehead—examine your face and write about what you see.

_____

_____

_____

_____

_____

_____

4.   Pick a person to observe and describe. Choose a stranger, so you can write without judging. How is she dressed? Do her purple suede boots and black felt hat reveal something about her personality? Watch the man by the bus stop. Notice how slowly he walks and the way he flicks his cigarette. Take note of people's shapes, sizes, clothing, perfume, and hair.

You may want to choose several people to watch. The more you do this, the more you'll discover how unique and fascinating we each are.

_____

_____

_____

_____

_____

_____

_____

5. Explore the rooms of your house or treatment center. If you're in the bathroom, let the water run and then listen. How would you describe that sound? Are there windows behind the shower? Is the floor soft with carpet or tiled, cool, and hard?

Go from room to room. Pay special attention to the senses you don't normally use. Smell the bedroom. Feel carpet with your hands. Try to use common words in uncommon combinations to capture the texture, or feeling, of each room.

_____

_____

_____

_____

_____

_____

_____

_____

_____

_____

_____

_____

_____

_____

_____

CHAPTER FOUR

Writing Through Anxiety

We're learning how to record the changes in our lives; we're taking note of new discoveries. But change can be stressful. New behavior and different ways of thinking bring with them the prospect of the unknown. How will our recovering lives unfold? We're familiar with a life of addiction. We're not familiar with sobriety or abstinence. Without addiction to buffer us, we feel the ups and downs of life (the texture of each day) keenly. We feel raw and exposed to everything: pain, joy, beauty, awe, and fear.

Writing can help keep us from becoming overwhelmed by all the change we're experiencing. Journaling probably isn't how we've handled anxiety in the past, but it can give us an outlet for our worries, a way to express fear or frustration. Writing allows us to record how anxiety operates in our journey of recovery, and ultimately, writing can help separate us from problems and feelings that seem threatening.

First, expression. How can journaling serve as an outlet for fear or anxiety? Easy! Outlet—let out. When we write, we let out fear. Instead of keeping anxiety bottled up inside of us, we throw the thoughts that frighten us onto paper. We know that bottled-up emotions can be dangerous. Those feelings have to go somewhere. One of those places can be paper. That doesn't mean we won't still feel angry, scared, or sad. But writing about our feelings is a way of acknowledging their existence. That acknowledgment— *I feel scared* or *angry* or *sad*—is an important act.

Naming what we're feeling can be a powerful experience. In the past, we've probably denied ourselves this simple act of self-affirmation. Have there been times when you hesitated to state exactly what you were feeling? Think back. Did you automatically respond, "I'm fine, everything's okay," the last time someone expressed concern about you? Probably. We all do this at times. We try to be polite, unobtrusive, and well-mannered. Quiet. But recovering people remain silent out of more than politeness.

We might not believe that we have the *right* to speak up about our thoughts or feelings, especially those feelings that are uncomfortable. Often, we feel a deep-rooted shame about *ourselves*. We're still not positive that we have a right to exist, let alone a right to have feelings! If we add this set of dynamics to societal rules about "good manners," we can silence ourselves completely.

Spend a couple of minutes thinking about times you've felt afraid. Did you tell anyone? Were you able to admit your fear to yourself? Describe the last time you hastily concealed your fear or anxiety, from yourself or someone else. Explore the reasons you remained silent. At this point in your journey of recovery, is it hard for you to acknowledge that your feelings are legitimate? Write a little bit about a time you hesitated to openly acknowledge your anxieties when someone expressed concern. Then, describe how you generally cope with anxiety at this point in your recovery.

People suffering from addictions often bury their real needs. We may have thought that our feelings of discomfort or unease weren't worth anyone's attention. Make no waves! Cause no commotion! But we *do* deserve to have our needs and feelings acknowledged. It doesn't matter if this isn't convenient for other people. How the people around us respond to our statements is up to them. It's our right and responsibility to name and acknowledge what we're feeling.

Of course, we can't forget that delicate balance between our feelings and another person's ability to respond to those feelings. Twelve Step groups, counselors, and friends can help us learn to negotiate the tricky terrain of asking for what we need from the people around us.

In this workbook, we're writing for ourselves. This is a personal record. The only risk you have to take here is with yourself! That may be enough for now. Make your own waves. When you're afraid, acknowledge that fear. If you're overwhelmed and exhausted, acknowledge that. There's relief in this process. It's a lot like standing up in a group and saying, "I'm an alcoholic," or "an overeater," or "an addict." We don't have to hide anymore.

Next time you're anxious or afraid, don't hide from yourself. Take out a piece of paper and write. Use the back of a check deposit slip or an old envelope from your desk—whatever is handy. Name what you're feeling. It doesn't have to be elaborate. Simply write over and over, "I'm afraid," or whatever fits for you at the moment. Or just write it once and use big block letters. Press hard and feel the pressure of your pen against the paper. Keep the paper with you. Allow yourself the power of those words. At this moment in your journey, this is how you feel. Say it. Write it. Try to do this each time you feel anxious or overwhelmed. Pretty soon you'll grow more comfortable acknowledging these feelings.

Not only does writing offer an initial outlet for fear, it can sometimes even ease that fear. Words are clues. Examining the words we use gives us insight into how we respond to different emotions. To see how this works, let's look at the phrase "I can't handle this." We've all heard someone say this, or we've said it to ourselves. But what does it mean to "handle" something? What clues can this phrase offer?

Handle means to hold on, to steer and direct. We say, "Get a hold of yourself!" or "I just can't get a handle on what I feel." Phrases like this reveal a lot about the nature of anxiety. When we say that we can't handle something, we feel a situation is out of our grasp. We're afraid something is beyond our ability to control or understand. Sometimes we can't handle things that are tangible—overdue bills, certain people, or particular places.

Other things we believe we can't handle come from inside: feelings that seem too intense, painful, or frightening. Sorrow and rage are good examples of emotions that seem too strong to handle. Just look at some of the words we use to talk about sorrow and rage. What clues do these words offer? We talk about "drowning in tears." We "give in," or succumb, to sorrow. These phrases create images of a self that is trapped or surrounded.

What about rage? Again, the words we use provide clues to understanding how we experience rage. We "fly into" or are "overcome with" rage. We "explode" with anger and "lose" our temper. Exploding? There goes our contained, centered self. The imagery is bomb-like: something is destroyed and scattered to the wind. It's the same when we "lose" our temper: the handle we have on our temper loosens and slips. Our grasp on the situation weakens, and our sense of control escapes.

When we feel a strong emotion like anger or sorrow, we fight that feeling. We battle against ourselves and feel afraid, in addition to feeling angry or sad or whatever else started the battle. Perhaps unaccustomed to the strength of these emotions, we're uncertain about how to respond. What can we do? Are we in charge or is the emotion? Frequently, the words we use to talk about emotions confuse the situation further. We start to feel like we're "drowning" or "exploding." Those are the directions our words provide.

Writing can help us change our responses to, and ideas about, those emotions. What words or phrases do you use to describe strong emotions? Here are some possibilities to explore: anger, sorrow, joy, fear, jealousy, pain. Add your own ideas to this list. Then, think about the particular words you use to describe these feelings. What images do you conjure up about your emotions? In the following space, make a list of emotions and then jot down some phrases that you use to describe each one.

_____

_____

_____

_____

_____

This list offers insight into how you respond to emotion. If you "sink" into sadness or "burst" with jealousy, your words may give you some clues for easing those sinking or bursting feelings. If you're bursting with anger, what can help you feel calm and contained? Think about the image that the word *burst* brings to mind. You might discover that wrapping yourself in an old cotton quilt makes you feel cocooned, safe. It helps calm the feeling of falling apart or exploding. Or you might decide to do "bursting" things that give you pleasure instead of anxiety. You can run around the block or dance hard to your favorite music. This process allows you to satisfy that need to explode or erupt—to act out what you're feeling in a manner *you* control.

Some of us may have found that the lists we made were pretty short. Maybe we had a tough time thinking of *any* words that describe emotion. Unaccustomed to acknowledging our emotions, we don't yet have the words to talk about how we feel. Our lack of a language for emotion is a clue, too. This shows us just how difficult it is for us to recognize and respond to emotion. We may have been ignoring strong feelings or pushing them aside.

If your list of emotions was very short (or nonexistent!), take some time to increase the number of words with which you're comfortable. How many different words can you think of for anger? *Fury, rage, mad, huff, ire.* In the space that follows, add some of your own.

_____

_____

_____

_____

Now, work on finding alternative words for the following emotions.

sad: _____

_____

happy: _____

_____

jealous: _____

_____

frightened: _____

_____

It's understandable that we might not have many words for emotions. After all, our feelings haven't been something we've talked about very much. The more we practice talking about emotions, the more words we'll have available to do so.

If you were able to list and describe your emotions, spend some time now matching the emotions you just described to some things that counteract or ease those emotions. Let the words guide you. Explore the complexity of the words and phrases you've written, just as we explored the word *handle* earlier. Use this understanding of words to find the pleasures that will allow you to sink or explode or fall apart in a comfortable way. Or find pleasures that counteract those feelings. Think of ways to soften yourself when you're hardened by envy; list possibilities for feeling slow instead of frantic, quiet instead of crazed.

EMOTION   PLEASURE

_____   _____

_____   _____

_____   _____

_____   _____

_____   _____

_____   _____

_____   _____

Writing gives us something visible. When we write, intangible feelings turn into something concrete. Words on paper—here's something we can hold, something we can handle. In the midst of emotional turmoil, there's strength in being able to order words, to control their direction. It's easier to grapple with what we can see. That's what we've been doing in this section—grappling with words, digging into their different meanings. This gives us insight into ourselves.

Also, writing about emotions serves as a reminder that *we are not* our emotions. Say we feel frightened. We can take that feeling and put something down on paper: *scared.* Then we read the word. That one word does not define who we are, no matter how intense or strong the feeling is. We each feel afraid from time to time. But it's a feeling—like every other feeling—that passes. In the space below, jot down a couple of words that describe how you feel right now. Are you anxious, tired, or happy? Choose one or two words that fit for you now. Write them down.

_____

_____

_____

_____

These words exist separately from you. There they are, on paper. While you experience anger or fear (or whatever you wrote), *you aren't* anger or fear. Separating ourselves from these words can serve to remind us that feelings come and go. They don't define who we are.

Most of us are still trying to figure out who we are and where our lives are heading. Recovery is uncharted territory. Life is filled with change. It's natural that we'll feel overwhelmed and afraid at times. But we can monitor, record, and reflect upon these feelings.

WRITING IDEAS

1. This exercise is another way to get a handle on anxiety and a reminder that you exist separately from your feelings.

Spend a few minutes listing all of your present worries. Write them down on a separate sheet of paper. Don't censor yourself. Be honest. List money concerns, recovery issues, or problems at work. If you're worried about dust under the bed, include that. No worry is too big or too small.

When you've finished, store the list in a file or drawer. Try to feel your anxiety slip into that drawer, too. Of course, problems don't disappear by magic. But you don't need to carry them around all day! You wouldn't carry that sheet of paper everywhere, would you? Imagine yourself carrying that list around—from the breakfast table to work to an evening Twelve Step meeting.

The paper would be an inconvenience. It would get in your way while you steered the car and ate dinner. Worry operates like this, too. We tend to carry our worries around. They keep our minds stuck; too often, all we can think about are our worries. It's tough at first, but try to keep your worries stored with that list.

Next, set aside a block of time to worry. At 8:00 P.M. sharp, get out the list. Now let yourself worry. Spend some time just fretting and feeling anxious. Taken together, the problems listed may seem insurmountable.

Then pick one or two of your worries and explore solutions. As we've done in this chapter, describe the problem in detail. Look at the words you've used and see if you can unpack hidden meanings or solutions in those words.

Allow yourself to write everything that pops into your mind. If you're worrying about money, maybe the thought of a surprise bonus at work keeps tugging at your mind. Write that down as a possible solution. We're accustomed to anticipating the worst. We expect disaster to drop from the sky. What about anticipating the best? Unexpected *wonderful* things happen, too!

When the allotted time is up, return the list to the drawer. Remember to allow your anxiety to stay with the list. You can return to the worry later. It's not something you need all day!

If you want, work on your list of worries once every day. Or, you can do it once, twice, or three times a week. Choose a block of time that fits your needs, too. It's up to you. Just try to keep those worries contained on paper; those problems exist separately from you.

2. The next time you're feeling overwhelmed, use the space at the end of this section to write about how anxiety affects your body. When you feel stressed, are you plagued by stomachaches? Maybe migraines keep you from thinking clearly or your chest tightens and stomach gurgles.

Move from head to toe, through your entire body. Try to slow down and take note of how your body responds to stress. This exercise can be calming, as well as instructive. It forces you to stop, observe, and record.

Sometimes our bodies respond to stress before we're conscious of feeling anxious! For example, the neck ache that returns each time you have coffee with an old friend might alert you to some hidden stress in that relationship. Use this exercise to observe the messages your body is sending.

CHAPTER FIVE

Discovering Your Writer's Memory

As we've seen, our interior journeys are exposing us to all kinds of new information. We're making discoveries about ourselves and about the world around us. For the first time in years, we may be enjoying a gorgeous sky, savoring evening silence, or catching the scent of burning autumn leaves. These are the details we generally overlook.

Even though we didn't take note of past skies and silences, we still experienced them. Countless details have gone into making us the people we are today. There are innumerable, tiny details of life that we experienced and can't recall. We may not remember it, but the smell of burning leaves floated through a night or two of our childhood. Each day of our lives passed under a unique sky. Countless colors presented themselves to us. We drank water. As children, we ate chocolates, string beans, oatmeal. We dug our toes into grass and sand.

Somewhere, deep in our unconscious, lie the patterns of our past. Some details we may be able to recall: the exact shade of a favorite blanket, the thick brick fence in front of a neighbor's yard, or the desk in a fifth-grade classroom. Most of us will remember people and events more easily than we'll remember fences and blankets. The first funeral we attended still sobers us. We remember the eighth-grade dance and how Chris hid under a table.

How do these memories relate to charting our interior journeys? Let's consider for a moment what one writer has to say about memory and writing. These are the words of the poet Rainer Maria Rilke:

> In order to write . . . one must see many cities, and people and things; one must get to know animals and the flight of birds, and the gestures that flowers make when they open to morning. One must be able to return to roads in unknown regions, to unexpected encounters, to partings long foreseen; to days of childhood that are still unexplained . . . to days spent in rooms withdrawn and quiet. . . .

> There must be memories of many nights of love, each unlike the
> others, of the screams of women in labor, and of women in childhood,
> light and blanched and sleeping, shutting themselves in. But one must
> also have sat beside the dead in a room with open windows and fitful
> noises.*

Of course, Rilke doesn't mean that these are the exact experiences we
need to have had in order to write. Witnessing birth or passing a dark night
with the dead is a pretty extraordinary event. But Rilke doesn't limit himself
to describing events. He talks about the details, too—the flight of birds and
the gestures of morning flowers.

What Rilke *is* telling us is that we write out of the sum of all experience.
To be alive means to experience pain, mystery, passion, and fear. Some
memories we recall with ease and pleasure; others can be touched only with
sorrow. As a poet, Rilke understood that the moment he picked up a pen, the
pain and pleasure of his past was the well from which he drew. All of Rilke's
varied experiences were important; they made him the man that he was.

Think of memory and the unconscious as containers for the entire world
we've walked through—the sidewalk stretching out from our childhood
homes, the narrow sleeping bag at slumber parties, the songs we sang at
church. These details exist along with the larger events of the past to make
each of us unique. Each of us has stories that only we can tell. Think of
these stories as coming from your *writer's memory*.

Memory is a difficult word. We may immediately associate memory with
addiction or the problems that preceded addiction. We look through our
personal histories, and we return to pain, anger, and sorrow. The pain of our
pasts is most likely a central focus in our recovery. We often need the
support of friends, and the guidance of our Higher Power, to help us work
through the emotions that memories evoke.

But there's another aspect of memory: memory is knowledge. Rilke
presents memory as what we must have "in order to write." He urges us to
"return to days of childhood," to the cities we've strolled through and the
people we've met. For Rilke, memories are more than the emotions they
evoke. Memory is a resource for writing. A writer's memory contains
forgotten details; it contains the texture of past days, the subtleties and
nuances of a life.

We dip into this memory each time we write. If we're asked to describe a
fence, the impressions of past fences are sources for what we write today.

---

* Rainer Maria Rilke, quoted in "The Poet in the World," by Denise Levertov, in *Woman as
Writer*, ed. Joan Grumman (Boston: Houghton Mifflin, 1978), 87.

Let's explore this idea using a candle. In the space that follows, describe a candle. What image comes to mind when you read the word *candle*? Is that image from a Christmas card or from the candle in your dining room? It may be a synthesis of many different candles you've seen or imagined in the past. Go ahead and describe a candle.

_____

_____

_____

_____

_____

_____

_____

_____

_____

_____

How did you *know* what to write? You know how to describe candles because you've seen them throughout your life! Consciously or unconsciously, what we've discovered yesterday finds its way into our writing today. Yesterday's sorrow will help us find the words for sorrow we experience today. We understand sorrow. We've experienced pain. We can write from that understanding and experience.

But we must be gentle with ourselves when we tap into this writer's memory. Sure, push a little and dig deep. Be creative with words and try to capture feelings on paper. Return to the cities and unexpected encounters of the past. But do this with compassion. We'll work toward accepting what we feel and toward writing without judgment. We can accept our pasts as knowledge.

Addiction cuts us off from self-knowledge. Now that we're recovering, we can turn inward and return to ourselves. Our interior journey leads us to self-knowledge, to the wisdom our pasts provide. This journey also returns us to the texture of our pasts and to the tiny details that filled each day. Remember, we write out of the sum of our life experience. All of our varied experiences are important; they make us the writers we are today.

WRITING IDEAS

1. What's your favorite color? Why? Recall memories of color—a deep blue from the sea of a childhood trip or the peach that colored an old bedroom wall. Create a story about how your favorite color has shown itself throughout your life, including now.

_____

_____

_____

_____

_____

_____

_____

2. What memories do you have of animals? From caged zoo tigers to the puppy you fed when you were nine, remember and write about the animals in your life. If you have no significant memories about animals, write about that fact. Why don't animals figure in your memories? Did you see animals in movies? Maybe you've never liked pets. Write about this.

_____

_____

_____

_____

_____

_____

_____

3.   How many pairs of shoes have you owned in your life? You probably have a favorite pair now. How do they match your personality? Think back to past shoes. Which ones did you love and wear thin? What about work shoes or shoes your parents made you wear? Write about the shoes you've owned.

_____

_____

_____

_____

_____

_____

_____

4.   Everyone has a relationship with breakfast. Some of us hate it; it's others' favorite meal. What do you like about breakfast now? When you were young, did you eat four bowls of sugary cereal in front of the TV on Saturday mornings? Gobble down Pop-Tarts while running off late to high school? Write about all of these breakfast habits and how they fit into your lifestyle at the time.

_____

_____

_____

_____

_____

_____

_____

_____

5. Did you have a best friend in grade school? Maybe you had a wild group of friends in college or found a soul mate in treatment. Write a brief history of the important friendships you've had.

_____

_____

_____

_____

_____

_____

_____

_____

_____

_____

_____

_____

_____

_____

_____

_____

CHAPTER SIX

Writing Toward Tomorrow

We've just delved into the past—into our writer's memory, where the details of each day are stored. It's this memory that we draw from each time we pick up a pen and face a clean sheet of paper. But what will happen when we face the future? Therein lies the most obviously uncharted territory that we will have to explore. Writing can help us prepare for the future. The stories we create can help us build a vision for our lives and direct the journey to come.

Creating a vision for the future means setting goals and making plans. This doesn't mean we'll *live* in the future. We live each day, one day at a time. But we know that yesterday and tomorrow frame today. Memory returns us to the past, and imagination leads us to the future. We imagine the future. We can hope, plan, and dream through writing.

This will be a new experience for many of us. Generally, as people suffering from addiction, we haven't developed the skill of long-range planning. Addiction sharply narrows our vision. But our ability to envision the future may have been limited long before we became consumed by addiction. Many of us didn't learn a lot about hope and vision in our childhood. From childhood through our years of addiction, we simply struggled to survive—to get through each day.

Think about what "the future" meant when you were young. At seventeen, what did you imagine life would be like as an adult? Did you have a vision of yourself attending college, working as a newspaper reporter, or raising children? What role models did you have, and what choices were available? Try to return to age seventeen and describe the vision you had of the future.

Most of our lives are quite different from those we imagined as teenagers. It's almost impossible to imagine what the future holds, no matter how old we are. Life is filled with surprises, tragedies, delights, and drama. So why plan? Anything can happen. We might inherit money, get a divorce, or move to Montana. Only one thing is certain: life is unpredictable.

But we are in control of *how we see ourselves!* That's the key to planning for, and writing toward, the future. A quick look at the Serenity Prayer can help clarify our thinking here.

> *God grant me the serenity*
> *To accept the things I cannot change,*
> *The courage to change the things I can,*
> *And the wisdom to know the difference.*

We accept the fact that we can't control the future. Our experiences will be countless and varied—some good, some not so good. Maybe our house will burn down. We might fall in love next week. Who knows? But we do know that we can change our attitude toward ourselves. We are in control of our self-image. So no matter what happens in the future, we can try to see and treat ourselves with love and respect.

With this in mind, return to the writing exercise you just did. At seventeen, was your vision of the future shaped by self-respect? Was there hope in what you wrote? Did you know what it meant to love and respect yourself when you were seventeen? Spend a couple of minutes in your writer's memory. Try to remember what you knew about self-respect when you were a teenager and describe that here.

At this point in our lives, we probably have a much stronger sense of what the words *respect* and *love* mean. After freeing ourselves from addiction, we may be applying those words to ourselves for the first time. We can apply those words to tomorrow, too. Picture yourself ten years from now. Think realistically and optimistically. Base this vision on love and respect; then fill in details. Give yourself a home, friends, and a job. Maybe you'll go to church on Sundays and have a vegetable garden. In this space, create a small story about the person you'll be in ten years. Keep one thing in mind: you deserve a full, happy life.

_____

_____

_____

_____

_____

_____

This vision will probably change as you change. However, your perception of yourself as a valuable person can remain at the center of your vision. The details—your job, home, friends—are less predictable. In fact, you can play with the details and create many different stories. You just wrote one; now try another. Create another version of your life in ten years. Give yourself a different job, enjoyable hobbies, and new friends.

_____

_____

_____

_____

_____

_____

Small stories like this help us shape our future by providing us with a particular vision toward which we can work. We don't need to limit the "future" to ten years from now, either. There's tomorrow to imagine. Before you go to bed tonight, use this space to describe your life tomorrow. Imagine moving through the day with confidence. How would it feel if you were to treat yourself with love and respect tomorrow? How would that look?

_____

_____

_____

_____

_____

_____

_____

Writing can help us create a strong, positive self-image. We can keep this image in mind when times get tough. Once in a while, we wake to a day we've been dreading. Maybe there's an unresolved conflict to be faced or a holiday that's always difficult. It's helpful to write about those days before they arrive. Picture yourself happy and healthy while you share a Thanksgiving dinner or resolve a conflict. Write a few paragraphs that feature you (sober or abstinent, treating yourself respectfully) moving through a day you anticipate will be difficult.

Many of us may not be used to creating positive pictures of the future. Instead, we're accustomed to expecting the worst; we assume tomorrow holds potential disaster and new problems to surprise us. These dim expectations can stem from the belief that we don't deserve to live comfortable, complete lives. Now that we're in recovery, we're learning that our lives are valuable! We each have the right to build a comfortable life. When we keep this in mind, our image of the future can be shaped by the foundation of happiness and health that we're building today.

Of course, the future will always be a little scary. That's the nature of uncharted territory. When we move into the unknown, we don't quite know what to expect. But at this point, we're experienced travelers. Throughout this whole workbook, we've been bravely charting new ground. In addition to exploring the territory of our interior lives, we've been using a new vehicle—writing—for this exploration. So the course of our journey has been twofold: we've learned about ourselves, and we've learned about writing. The two work well together. We can use everything we've learned about ourselves and about writing to create a vision for tomorrow.

We probably still have some anxieties about our journey. That's natural. Everyone feels afraid from time to time. Also, there's a lot of territory we've yet to cover because the journey of recovery is a lifelong process. Growing more comfortable with, and less anxious about, writing is a lifelong process, too. The fears we have about writing don't disappear overnight. Many of our fears are products of larger social attitudes; society continues to place "writing" in a special category where only artists, teachers, and professors are allowed. Sometimes we have to remind ourselves that writing is just a skill we learn, like driving.

We're slowly discovering that we each have the ability to write about our lives. When we write, we push ourselves to look a little harder and longer at the world around us. Not only are we making observations about the physical world, but we're making observations about our interior world as well. This isn't always an easy process. We occasionally find ourselves overwhelmed by everything we're observing and learning. Tapping into our writer's memory means occasionally bumping into old wounds.

But our writer's memory offers us much more than pain. It's there that the experiences of our lives are stored: small details and big events that make each of us unique. Think of the wealth that lies in our writer's memory! That's a place no one but we as individuals have access to. As recovering people, we share many concerns and goals. But as writers, we each have a unique story to tell.

Closing this workbook is an end to a small part of our journey. It's a single chapter in our lives as writers and recovering people. We know now that *we can write*. More important, we're learning that we deserve to write! We each deserve to have a voice and to tell our story. Our observations, about ourselves and the larger world, are valuable. The words we create are important.

Words can help direct our continuing journey of recovery. This workbook has offered us some basic instruction and has provided some structure for our writing, but we don't have to stop writing because we've finished reading it. The possibilities for writing (just like the possibilities for our lives) are endless. We can continue journaling and creating records. All we need to do is keep observing and taking note—of ourselves and of the world around us. That's exactly what we've been doing in this workbook, and we can continue to do this on our own. Writing can help direct and record our journey of recovery, but only time will tell where this journey leads us.

Only you can describe where you've been and who you are. Go ahead and let the next stage of the journey begin. Write about who you are today. It's time to write the story of your life, one day at a time.

WRITING IDEAS

Create your own writing exercises! You'll need more than the space that follows—you'll need dozens of notebooks and many years. It's the story of your interior journey.

_____

_____

_____

_____

_____

_____

_____

_____

_____

_____

_____

_____

_____

_____

_____

More titles that will interest you...

WomanWords
A Journal for My Self
    These open pages and thoughtful quotes encourage women to use
journaling as part of the recovery process. The flow of these pages
makes this an ideal graduation, anniversary, or "special-day" gift that
encourages journaling as a healing activity. 96 pp.
Order No. 8301

The Twelve Step Prayer Book - Second Edition
A Collection of Favorite Twelve Step Prayers and Inspirational Readings
    written and compiled by Bill Pittman
    If we're just beginning a life of recovery, or if we've been in the
program for a while, this collection of Twelve Step prayers provides us
with inspirational readings that enhance our spiritual growth. For those
of us who have trouble finding the "right words" to speak with our
Higher Power, these prayers may help us express our feelings. 136 pp.
Order No. 2367

For price and order information, or a free catalog,
please call our Telephone Representatives.

HAZELDEN

1-800-328-0098	**1-651-213-4000**	**1-651-213-4590**
(Toll Free, U.S., Canada,	(Outside the U.S.	(FAX)
and the Virgin Islands)	and Canada)	http://www.hazelden.org

Pleasant Valley Road • P.O. Box 176 • Center City, MN 55012-0176

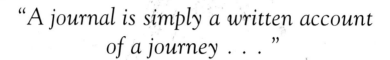

"A journal is simply a written account of a journey . . ."

Early explorers used journals as a way to trace their travels. This journal is no different. It's a tool for exploring and making discoveries about the uncharted territory of your personal recovery from addiction.

Explaining how journal-writing and recovery can work together, this workbook—for and about writing—offers you a way to increase your self-awareness. It carefully guides you through the journaling process by encouraging you to write your own story. It helps you get beyond grammar, punctuation, and the block many people have about writing to freely write about what you know best: your own experiences.

People have been exploring uncharted territories and writing about their explorations for years. This journal is your chance to embark on your own interior journey. "Home, to ourselves, is where we're headed."

HAZELDEN®

hazelden.org
800-328-9000

ISBN 978-0-89486-935-8

50795

9 780894 869358

USA $7.95

Order No. 8330

Coaching Football's
3-3-5 DEFENSE

LEO HAND AND RICK MOLINA